Under the Sea

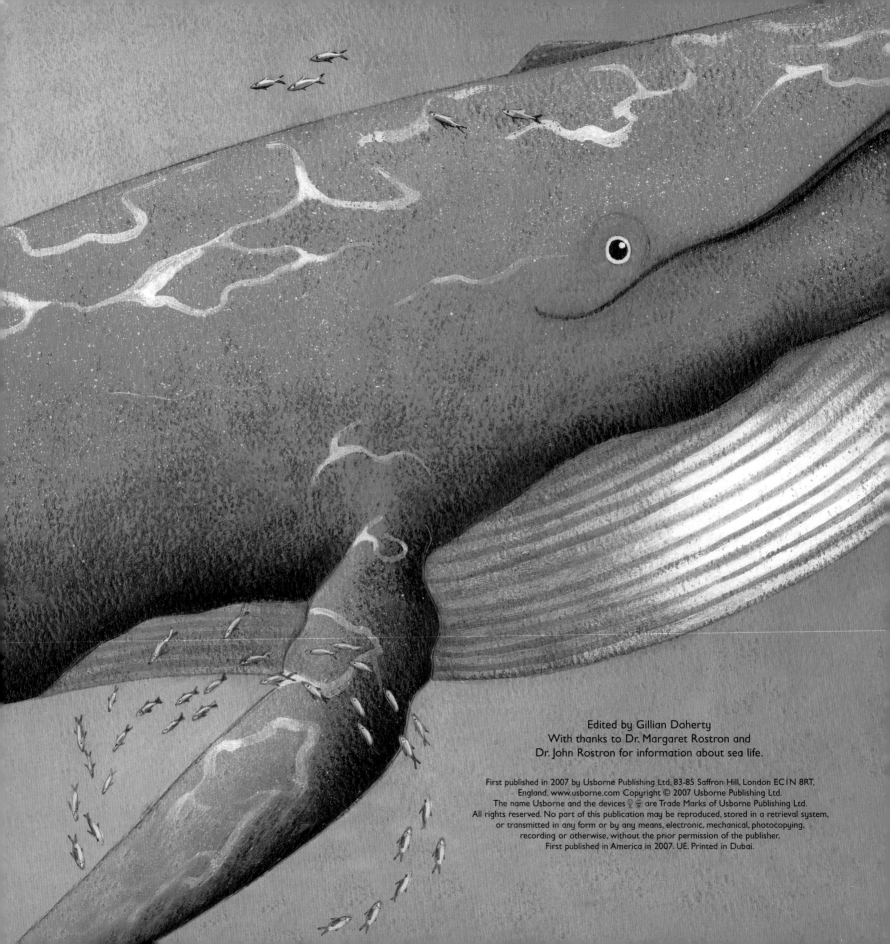

Edited by Gillian Doherty
With thanks to Dr. Margaret Rostron and
Dr. John Rostron for information about sea life.

First published in 2007 by Usborne Publishing Ltd. 83-85 Saffron Hill, London EC1N 8RT,
England. www.usborne.com Copyright © 2007 Usborne Publishing Ltd.
The name Usborne and the devices ♀ ⊕ are Trade Marks of Usborne Publishing Ltd.
First published in America in 2007. UE. Printed in Dubai.

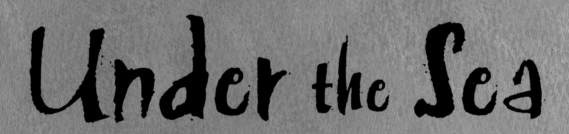

Under the Sea

Anna Milbourne

Illustrated by Cathy Shimmen

Designed by Nicola Butler

The sea is so big it reaches all around the world.
In each place it's as different as can be.

Near a sunny shore, where the water is warm,
there are hundreds of jewel-bright fish.

They bustle around the coral reef
nibbling at teeny-tiny plants.

A turtle swims along
and settles on the seabed...

...where lots of eager, yellow fish
crowd around to clean its shell.

At night, the fish tuck themselves
into nooks and crannies to go to sleep.

A hungry eel slinks out
of its hole to hunt.

Any creature it finds
might become a midnight snack!

When morning comes, the eel skulks home,
and other creatures roam around.

In an underwater meadow,
sea cows munch on long sea grass.

A group of rays
swims slowly by.

They flap their wings as though they're flying
and glide out into the open sea.

Imagine sailing across the wide, blue sea.
There's nothing but water for miles and miles.

Then suddenly beneath you swims
the **biggest** creature there's ever been.

It's a gentle giant — a big blue whale.
He's searching for other whales.

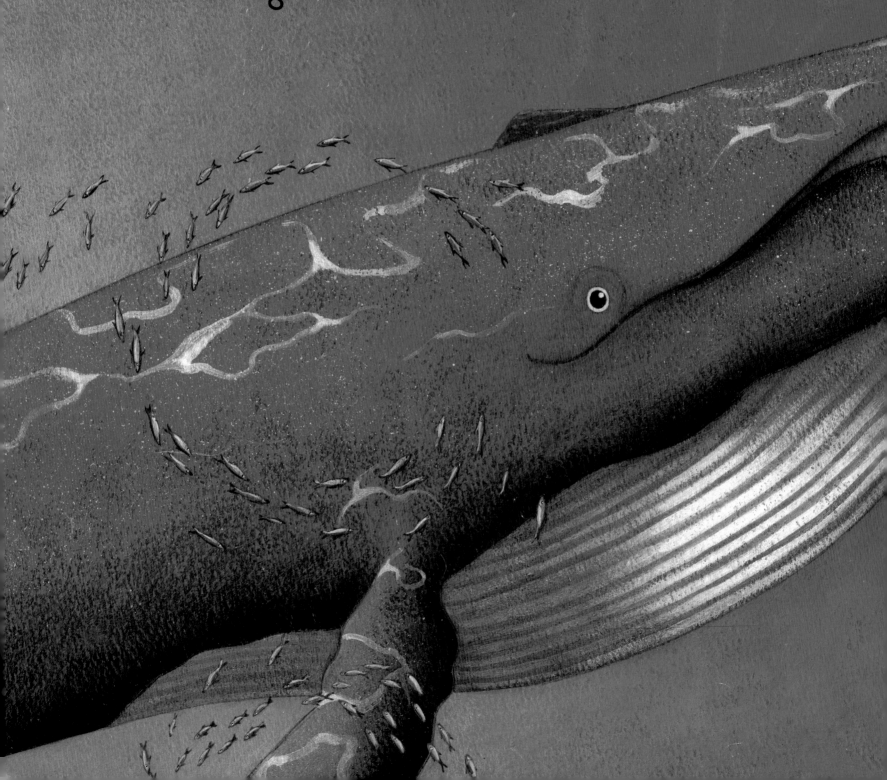

He sings a booming, lonely song
into the empty blue.

From far away across the sea,
another whale's song comes floating back.

Out here, far from any shore, the sea is VERY deep.

It gets darker and darker
the deeper you go.

Then, all at once,
twinkling lights appear.

All kinds of strange and pretty creatures are flashing messages in the dark.

It takes hours to get
to the bottom of the sea.

People have been there
in little submarines.

They found mountains and valleys,
just like you see on land.